TIGRINYA CHILDREN'S BOOK

Alice in Wonderland
(English and Tigrinya Edition)

WAI CHEUNG

This page intentionally left blank.

ABOUT THE BOOK

Raise your children in a bilingual fashion with this bilingual coloring book that captures the magic and beauty of Alice in Wonderland's story along with a dual language storytelling that is perfect for parents who want to raise their children in a bilingual environment.

CONTENTS

Alice saw the White Rabbit pause for a moment to check the time on his pocket-watch.

አሊስ ነጩን ጥንቸል ላየችው ሰዓቱን ለማየት ባስቆ ሰዓት ላይ የምርመራ ጊዜ እንድን መውሰዱ አስቦ ከእሱ ልብሱ ኪስ በተወጠ ድፍራ በለ ጊዜው ፊት ከጊዜ እንድን መውሰዱ በሰ።

Plate 1.
Rabbit

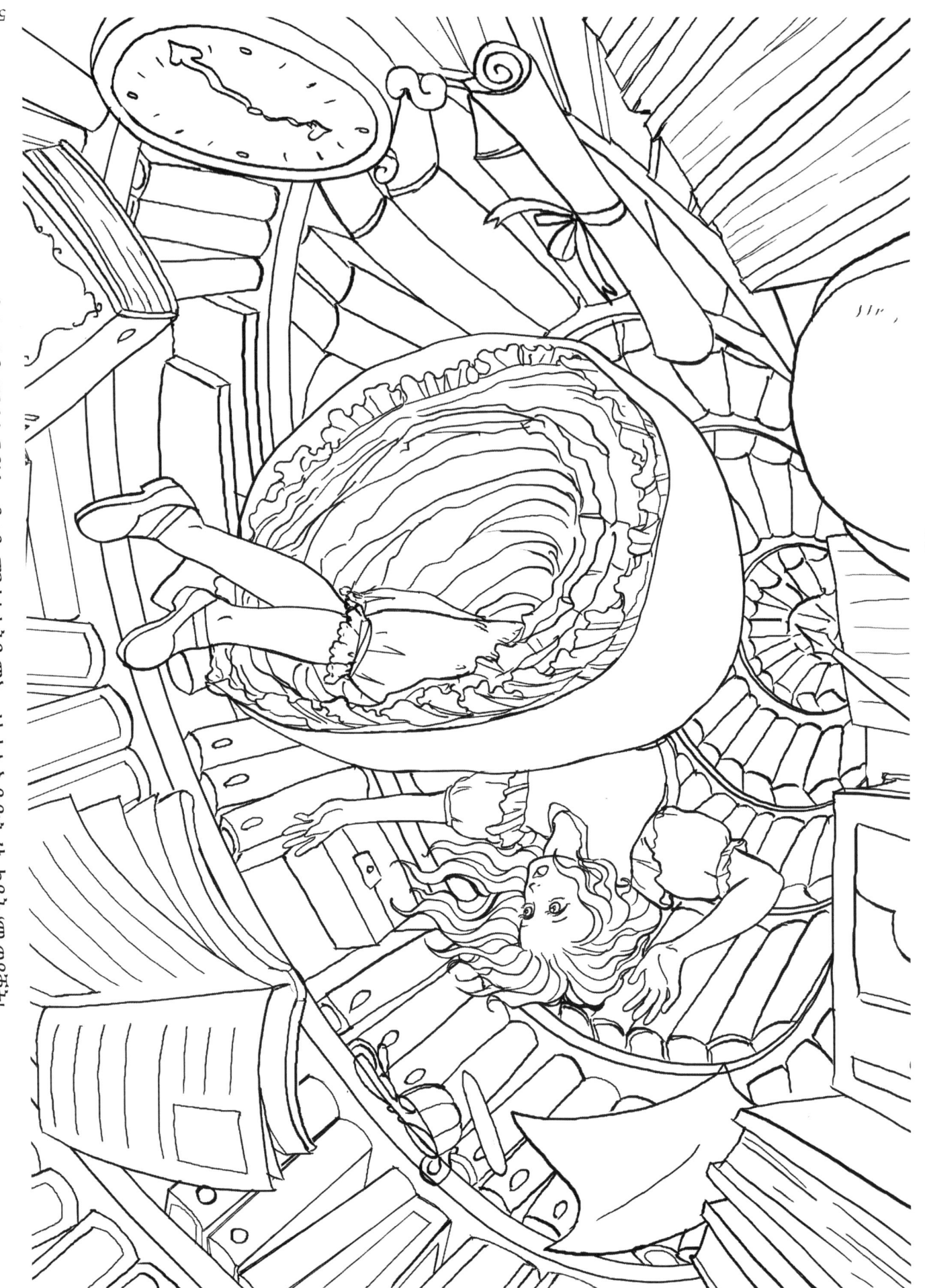

When the White Rabbit disappeared down a rabbit hole, Alice followed — and fell!

አስ ዐያዶ ማንዣፋ ናብ'ቲ ጉድጓድ ማንከራ አተዊ ምኽባብ ኣቢሳ ደሓሪኣ ከይዳ 'ሞ ወደቐት!

Plate 2.
Falling

Alice finally stopped falling, so she began to walk and encountered the Caterpillar.

አሊስ መውደቋን አስቁማ ንትተ ምውራድ መዘው እስከ ተቀ ፀምቧሳልሙ ክትርኳስ ምባም ጀመርት።

Plate 3.
The Caterpillar

She next met and looked up at the large grin of the Cheshire Cat.

ቀጥላ ከዛ ጋር ገጠመ ፊት ጀባር ይደው ማስረጫትዋ ገን ብርሆ በለ::

Plate 4.
Cheshire Cat

Alice had tea with the very mad March Hare and Hatter, as well as the sleepy Dormouse.

አሊስ ከጅብ ማርች ሃርና ከኮፍያ ሰሪው ዕብዶች ጋር፣ ሻይ ጠጣች፣ እንዲሁም እንቅልፋም ከሆነው አይጥ ጋር።

Plate 5.
Tea Party

After the tiring tea party Alice saw three playing cards standing under a rose bush, ready to paint the white roses red.

በዲ ሻይ አቲ መዳና'ከጎ፥ (መስልቸዉ) ሳይ ሻ፤ ፖርት አለሳ አስ ተስተ ር፤ ሰሳር ዘለዋ ዴር ጠመዉ አስን ከተክሰን ዐፈ፤ ዕምበበታት ቀይሳ ሰሳር ከከሰብ መከሳናታ ሰክፍታት ርዳየታን።

Plate 6.
Painting Roses

Alice soon met the Queen of Hearts, who was quick to yell, "Off with her head!"

አሊስ ንግሥቲቱ ዘተዛወለፑ ንባሰቱ ልባያቱ ሪዳያቱሙ "ስርአሳ አባል ወቸዐታ፡፡"

Plate 7.
The Queen

All the madness that lie at the bottom of the rabbit hole swirled around Alice in a dream-like whirlwind...

ሁሉም መወራጀት ከባ አቢስ ወዳሽ ኢት ጋድጋፍ ማታለል ከፈት ከም ሕልም አለ አይስ ክበብ ጥበብ ቅ ወያ ከሱ ከም ሕም አውሎ ነፋስ ተበሱ ።

Plate 8.
The Cards

ABOUT THE BOOK

Raise your children in a bilingual fashion with this bilingual coloring book that captures the magic and beauty of Alice in Wonderland's story along with a dual language storytelling that is perfect for parents who want to raise their children in a bilingual environment.

This page intentionally left blank.

Printed in Great Britain
by Amazon

Printed in Great Britain
by Amazon

This book comes with a free printable PDF version so you can print another one when you are done with this one!

Go to

LiltKids.com/download-95333

to download it.

Cat Stress Relieving Designs & Patterns
Adult Coloring Book
Illustrated by Ananta Vishnu

Inspirational Quotes
A Positive & Uplifting
Adult Coloring Book

Illustrated by Mariya Stoyanova

Incredible India Coloring Book For Adults
Illustrated by Ananta Vishnu

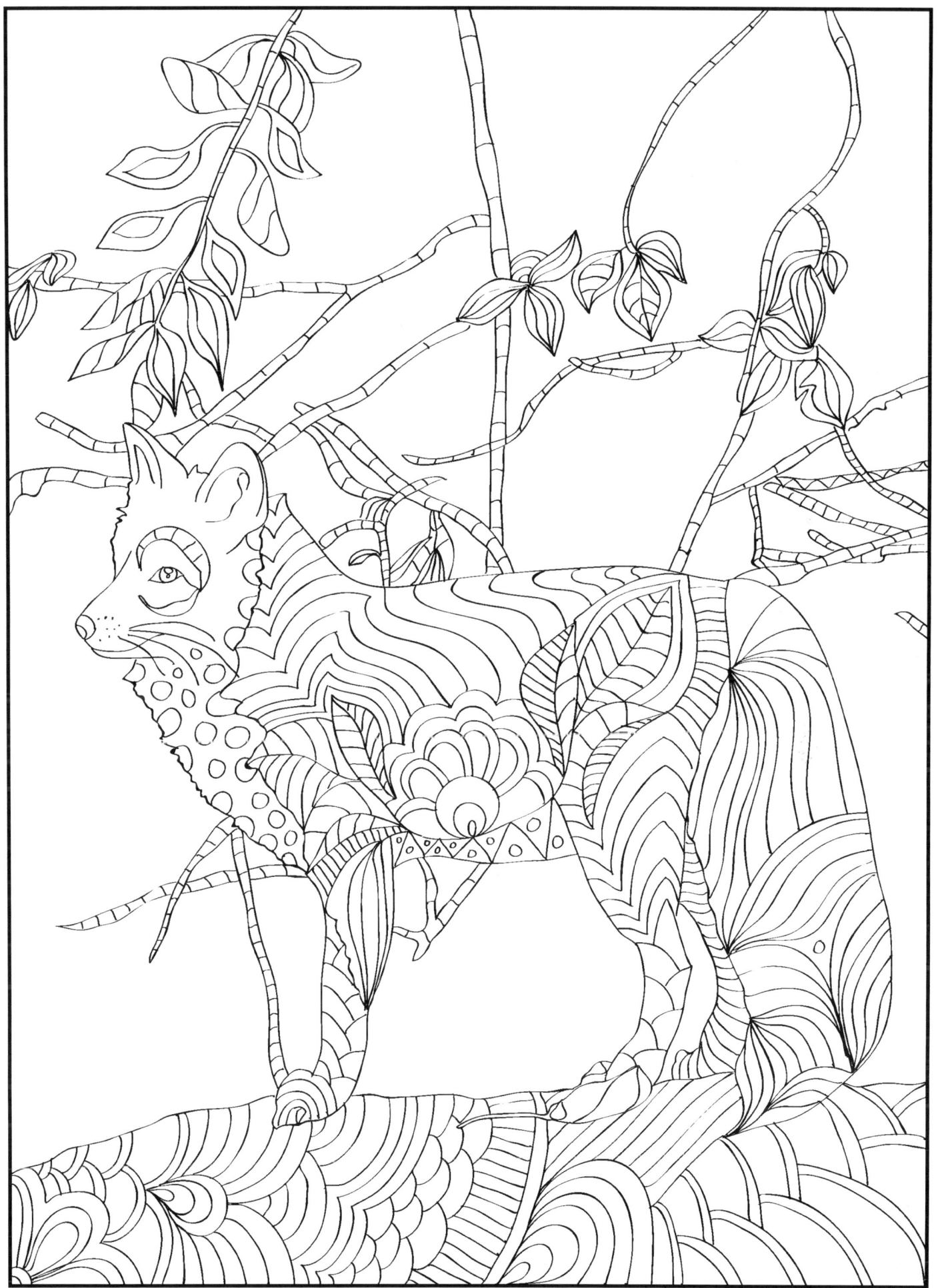

Animal Adult Coloring Book
Nature Patterns for Creativity & Calm
Illustrated by Petya Kazantseva

Animal Adult Coloring Book
Stress Relieving Patterns & Designs
Illustrated by Anastasiia Nikitina

IN MY ENGLISH GARDEN
Beautiful Illustrations For Adults Color

OCEAN FANTASY
Beautiful Mermaid Coloring Book For Adults & Children

OCEAN FANTASY:

Beautiful Mermaid Coloring Book
For Adults & Children

COLORING INSPIRATIONAL QUOTES
The Uplifting Coloring Book For Adults

Coloring Inspirational Quotes:
The Uplifting Coloring Book For Adults

MAGIC OCEAN ADVENTURE
Adult Coloring Book

MAGIC IN THE GARDEN
The Whimsical Adult Coloring Book

"Enjoy free bonus images from some of our best-loved coloring books on the next few pages."

Find our books on Amazon.

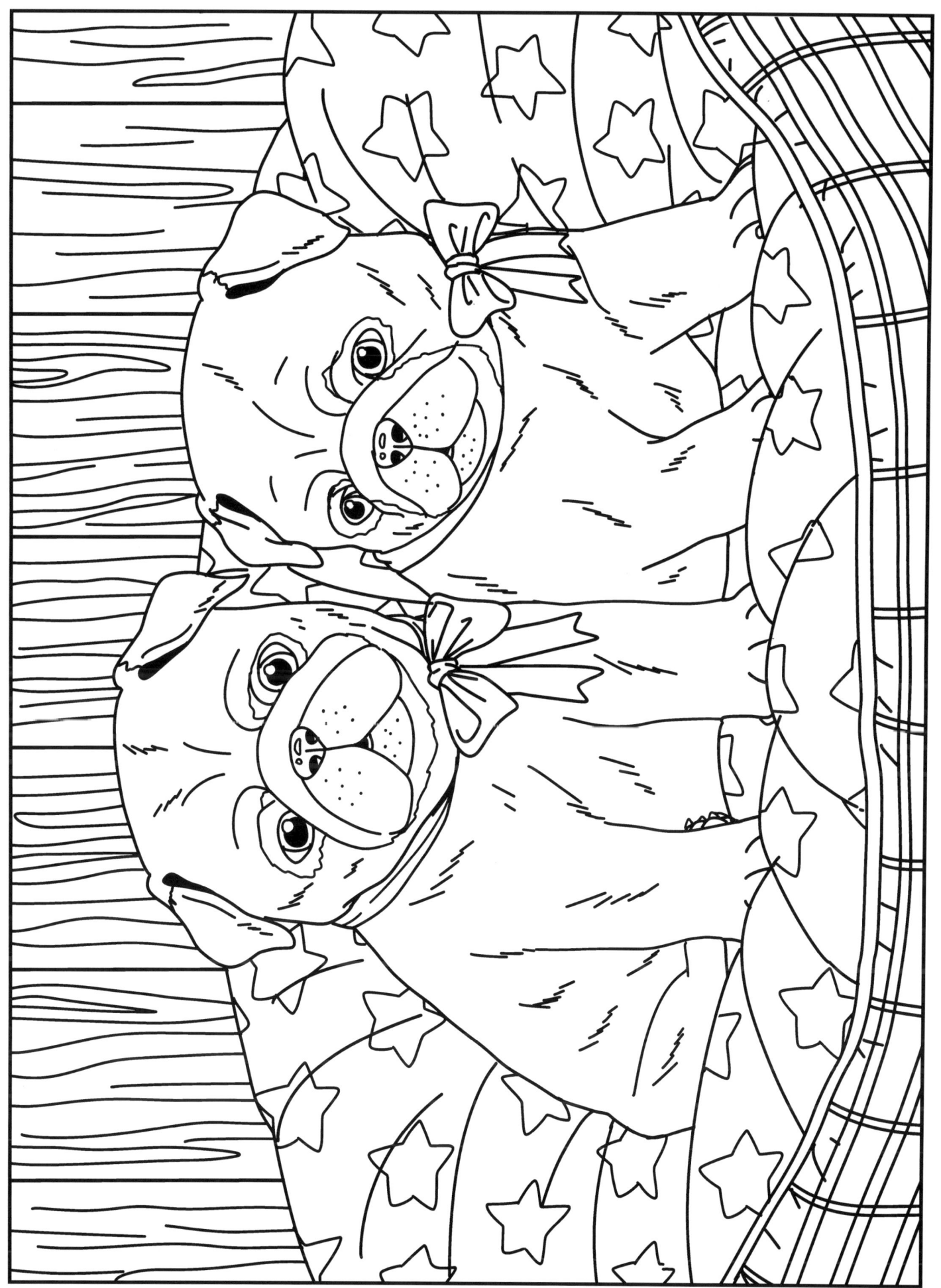

• COLORING TIPS •

1) Relax & Enjoy:
Coloring is good for stress relief, anxiety, depression, and so much more. There's no wrong way to color. You can do it while you watch television, listen to music, drink tea, or while you do nothing but focus on your coloring. Don't compare your finished product to anyone else's. You'll improve the longer you keep at it, and you probably won't love every single image you create. That's okay! If you are enjoying the journey, that's all that matters.

2) Choose the right tools:
Colored pencils, crayons, markers, oh my! What you choose to color with is a very personal choice. Visit LiltKids.com/tools for a rundown of our favorite brands. If you choose markers, we recommend you put a blank sheet of paper behind your page so that the colors don't run through onto the next image.

3) Color schemes:
Try out your colors in the test pages at the beginning of this book, and pick out some that might go well together. If you also google "color scheme", you will find an abundance of websites for inspiration.

4) Getting the pages out of your book:
Unfortunately, we don't yet have the ability to offer perforated pages in our books. However, you can find a tool called a page perforator on amazon.com for under $4, and turn any coloring book page into a perforated page!

5) Share your work:
We want to see what you color! So do our illustrators. Snap a photo and show us your work. Go to LiltKids.com, and click on the social media link of your choice: facebook, twitter, instagram, or pinterest.

Or email it to us and we'll share it for you!

LiltKidsColoring@gmail.com

Really, we want to see it.

We hope you enjoy this book!
If you do, please consider leaving a review on
Amazon.com, it really helps us out.

COLOR TEST PAGE

COLOR TEST PAGE

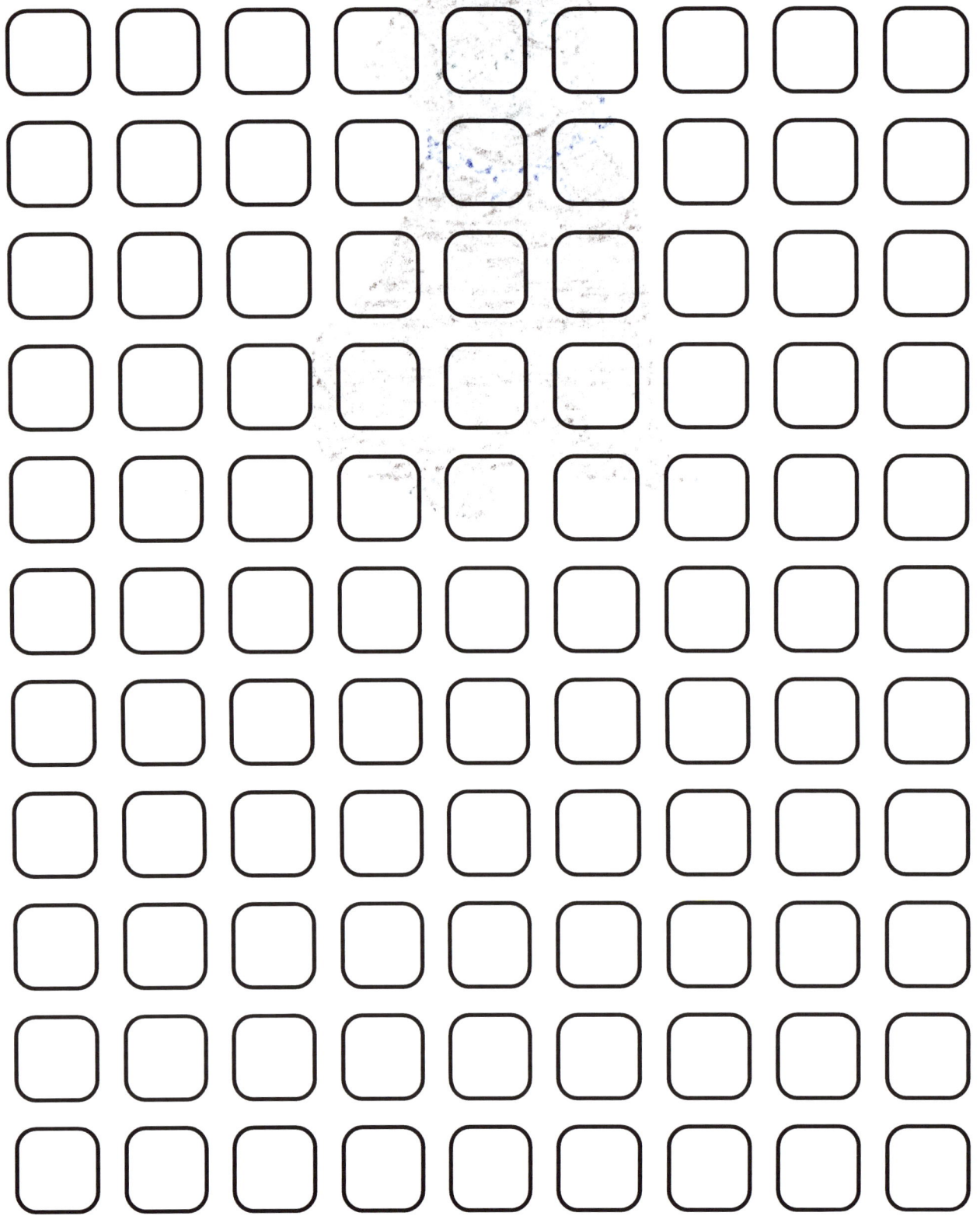

I Love Pugs Coloring Book

Illustrated by: Jean Tumbagahan

By Lilt Kids Coloring Books